LEMURS, LORISES, AND OTHER LOWER PRIMATES

A TRUE BOOK

by

Patricia A. Fink Martin

Children's Press®
A Division of Grolier Publishing

New York London Hong Kong Sydney
Danbury, Connecticut

A red-ruffed lemur

Reading Consultant
Linda Cornwell
*Coordinator of School Quality
and Professional Improvement
Indiana State Teachers Association*

Content Consultant
Kathy Carlstead, Ph.D.
*National Zoological Park
Washington, D.C.*

The photograph on the cover shows a brown lemur. The photograph on the title page shows a Senegal bushbaby.

Visit Children's Press® on the Internet at:
http://publishing.grolier.com

Library of Congress Cataloging-in-Publication Data

Martin, Patricia A. Fink, 1955–
    Lemurs, lorises, and other lower primates / by Patricia A. Fink Martin.
        p. cm. — (A true book)
    Includes bibliographical references and index.
    Summary: Describes several species of lower primates, including the lemur, aye-aye, galago, loris, and tarsier, and their endangered status.
    ISBN: 0-516-21575-2 (lib. bdg.)   0-516-27015-X (pbk.)
    1. Prosimians —Juvenile literature. [1. Prosimians. 2. Endangered species.] I. Title. II. Series.
QL737.P9M37   2000
599.8'3—dc21
                                                                99-17066
                                                                CIP
                                                                AC

Contents

A monkey (left) and a chimpanzee (right) are primates.

Prosimians: The Lower Primates

You belong to a special group of animals called primates. Gorillas, chimpanzees, and monkeys are primates too. Humans and chimpanzees have lived on Earth for a long time. But some primates have been around even longer.

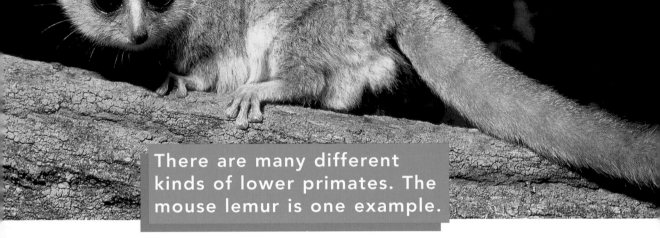

There are many different kinds of lower primates. The mouse lemur is one example.

Scientists call them prosimians, or lower primates.

Some lower primates are as small as squirrels. Others are as big as house cats. Fur covers their bodies and long tails. They have long, pointed noses and big eyes. Their eyes look

This slow loris is a lower primate. It lives in Asia.

Look carefully at the hands of this red-fronted lemur. They have four fingers and a thumb.

forward, so they can tell whether objects are nearby or far away.

Prosimians are like other primates in one important way. They have hands that can grasp things. Their hands are not like the paws of a dog or a cat. They have four thin fingers and a thumb set apart from the fingers. Their hands are perfect for grasping and holding tree limbs or small objects.

This black-and-white ruffed lemur moves through the trees like a monkey.

Not Quite Monkeys

Prosimians live in Africa and Asia. They can also be found on an island called Madagascar. Some move through the trees like monkeys. But prosimians cannot use their fingers as well as monkeys.

Monkeys can pluck insects and dirt from their fur with

their fingers. Prosimians cannot do this. They clean their
fur with their teeth. Their
lower teeth act like a built-in
comb.

Monkeys use their eyes to
get around. Many prosimians
are active at night. Sight is

Crowned lemurs help
each other keep their
fur clean.

This Philippine tarsier's big eyes help it hunt at night.

important to them. But they also use their ears and noses to understand the world.

Some lower primates produce smelly liquids. They use these to mark trees. The smell tells others to stay away.

Ring-tailed lemurs have long tails covered with rings of black and white fur.

The Ring-tailed Lemur

The ring-tailed lemur lives on Madagascar, an island off the southeast coast of Africa. Most of this lemur's body is covered with tan fur. Patches of black and white mark its face. But it is the tail that you really notice. Rings of black and white fur cover its long bushy tail.

The ring-tailed lemur is the king of stink. Its tail is an important weapon. But only the male lemurs defend themselves in this way. A bad-smelling substance is pro-duced by a gland on each wrist. The lemur rubs the sub-stance—and the smell—into the fur of its tail. When the tail is ready, up it goes like a shot. The lemur waves its tail

When a lemur feels threatened, it raises its tail. No enemy can stand the stink!

up and down like a flag. The odor drifts with the wind. The enemy takes one sniff and runs away!

Lemurs spend most of their time in small groups called troops.

These lemurs spend a lot of time on the ground. They travel in small groups called troops. A troop spends its day feeding, grooming, and resting. The lemurs search the trees for their favorite foods—fruits.

The World's Smallest Primate

More than twenty-five kinds of lemurs live on Madagascar. Unlike the ring-tailed lemur, many are active at night. Their big eyes help them see in the dark.

Even in daylight, the gray mouse lemur would be hard

to spot. This lemur weighs no more than a letter from your mailbox. At 2 ounces (57 grams), the gray mouse lemur is the world's smallest primate.

The gray mouse lemur is a tiny animal.

The gray mouse lemur's large eyes and ears help it hunt at night.

The gray mouse lemur lives in forests. At night, it hunts for food among the trees. It runs along branches on its tiny legs. Its big ears pick up the sounds of its prey— insects, small lizards, and frogs. It also eats fruits and leaves. During the day, the little lemur sleeps in a tree hole. Sometimes it makes a nest of dead leaves.

During the mating season, males and females pair up. Later, twins are born. For the first few weeks, their mother carries them everywhere. Most primate mothers carry their babies in their arms, but the gray mouse lemur carries her babies in her mouth!

How many lemurs can you spot in this photograph? Look carefully.

The Aye-aye

Of all the primates, the aye-aye looks the strangest. It is almost hard to believe an aye-aye is a primate! Its body is covered with long black fur with white tips. Most aye-ayes are about the size of a raccoon. Glowing orange eyes stare out from its face.

Look at this aye-aye's eyes and ears. Do you think it is active during the day or at night?

Large bat-like ears stick out from the sides of its head. Its long fingers seem bony and twisted. Each finger has a sharp, curved claw. Only the big toe of each foot ends in a flat nail.

Because people have killed so many aye-ayes, there are very few left in the world. Aye-ayes are endangered species.

Where can you find this animal? Outside of a zoo, you'd have to travel to Madagascar. Some people

there are afraid of aye-ayes.
They believe aye-ayes can
bring a curse. They often kill
the animals on sight.

Aye-ayes are quiet and blend in with their surroundings. Even if you were looking right at an aye-aye, you might not see it.

The aye-aye is just an animal. It has no special powers. The aye-aye lives alone in the forest. It eats insects that tunnel under tree bark. To find insects, the aye-aye taps on a tree branch and listens. A hollow sound may mean hidden food. With its sharp teeth, the aye-aye bites through the bark. It stabs the prey with its long bony fingers, pulls out its catch, and stuffs the insect into its mouth.

The Loris

Lorises live in the forests of Southeast Asia and India. They climb carefully through the trees, moving one leg at a time. Their hands and feet act like clamps. Each grabs tightly to a branch. They can even climb down a tree head first!

Lorises spend most of their time in trees. They use their eyes and nose to find prey).

Lorises are active at night. Their big eyes can gather more light than our smaller eyes. Lorises also depend on their nose to tell them when dinner is close by. These primates eat fruits, insects, and birds' eggs. They catch their prey with stubby fingers.

Lorises mark trees with urine to keep track of one another.
    The loris lives alone in the forest. It sleeps in a tree with its feet clamped around a branch and its body rolled up into a furry ball.

This loris is grooming its fur.

This galago lives in a national park in South Africa.

The Galago

The galago lives in Africa. This little animal has large round eyes and a round face. The largest galagos are as big as a squirrel. The smallest are the size of a chipmunk. The call of a galago sounds like a human baby crying. That is why many people call this primate a bushbaby.

A bushbaby listens closely for the sounds of insects.

Bushbabies are most active at night. They use their big eyes and ears to search for insects. When they hear a noise, they can turn each ear toward it. Bushbabies are good hunters. They can even catch gnats with their tiny hands.

Bushbabies are excellent jumpers.

If a bushbaby senses danger, it runs away. Bushbabies can run fast and can leap up to 15 feet (4.6 meters). They use their long back legs to jump from tree to tree.

Bushbabies live in a group, but they often hunt alone. Like lorises, bushbabies mark trees with urine to keep track of one another.

This little tarsier has just caught a grasshopper.

The Tarsier

Most lower primates eat leaves, fruits, and insects. But the tarsier is a meat eater. Lizards, large insects, bats, and birds are its favorite prey.

You might be surprised to hear that this fierce hunter is no larger than a chipmunk.

The tarsier lives in the forests of Southeast Asia.

In the darkness, the tarsier waits patiently for prey to pass by. It clings tightly to a tree trunk. The pads on its fingers and toes help the little animal to hold on.

Something is moving on the forest floor. The tarsier turns its large ears to hear it better. Then it twists its tiny head to catch sight of its prey—a lizard.

A tarsier waits patiently for prey to come its way.

Like the bushbaby, the
tarsier is a good jumper.

As tropical rain forests are destroyed, prosimians and other creatures that live there lose their homes.

To Find Out More

Here are some additional resources to help you learn more about lemurs, lorises, and other lower primates.

Books

Darling, Kathy. **Lemurs on Location.** Lothrop, Lee & Shepard Books, 1998.

Lasky, Kathryn. **Shadows in the Dawn: The Lemurs of Madagascar.** Harcourt Brace, 1998.

Martin, James. **Lemurs and Other Animals of the Madagascan Rain Forest.** Capstone Press, 1995.

Maynard, Thane. **Primates: Apes, Monkeys, and Prosimians.** Franklin Watts, 1994.

Tattersall, Ian. **Primates: Lemurs, Monkeys, and You.** Millbrook Press, 1995.

Organizations and Online Sites

Don't Call Me Monkey
http://www.tcfhe.com/ Dunston/Not/Content/ dontCallMe/index.html

Not all primates are monkeys. This site will teach you the difference between monkeys, prosimians, and great apes.

Duke University Primate Center
3705 Erwin Road
Durham, NC 27705
http://www.duke.edu/web/ primate/

International Primate Protection League
P.O. Box 766
Summerville, SC 29484
http://www.ippl.org

Living Lemurs
http://www.selu.com/~bio/ lemur/contents.html

This site features all kinds of information about and photos of lemurs as well as links to other interesting sites.

Rainforest Action Network
221 Pine Street, Suite 500
San Francisco, CA 94104
http://www.ran.org/kids _action/index.html

World Wildlife Fund
1250 24th Street, NW
Washington, DC 20037
http://www.wwf.org/

Important Words

endangered living things in danger of
  extinction

grooming picking dirt, insects, and
  dead skin from an animal's fur

prey an animal hunted and eaten by
  another animal

primate a type of mammal with eyes
  that face forward, hands that grasp,
  and a large brain

prosimian a type of primate that may
  be active at night and may depend
  on its senses of smell and hearing
  more than sight

troop a small group of animals of the
  same kind that feed, sleep, and
  travel together

urine a liquid waste passed out of the
  body

Index

(**Boldface** page numbers
indicate illustrations.)

Meet the Author

Patricia A. Fink Martin has a doctorate in biology. After working in the laboratory and teaching for 10 years, she began writing science books for children. *Booklist* chose her first book, *Animals that Walk on Water*, as one of the ten best animal books for children in 1998. Dr. Martin lives in Tennessee with her husband, Jerry, and their daughter, Leslie.